HOW TO OPEN A SUCCESSFUL
PIZZERIA

A Comprehensive Guide to Starting, Running and Growing Your Own Pizzeria Venture

ROGER LOONEY

Copyright Notice

This book is copyrighted in 2019-2022 by Dan & Elbert Associates.

All rights reserved.
Its content may not be copied or duplicated in part or whole by any means without express prior agreement in writing

TABLE OF CONTENTS

Chapter 1: Introduction	**5**
Chapter 2: Crafting Your Concept	**7**
Finding Your Niche in the Pizza Market	7
Deciding on Your Menu and Specialties	8
Designing Your Unique Selling Proposition	10
Chapter 3: Market Research and Planning	**13**
Analyzing the Local Market	13
Understanding Your Target Audience	14
Creating a Business Plan	16
Chapter 4: Legalities and Regulations	**19**
Navigating Permits and Licenses	19
Complying with Health and Safety Standards	20
Understanding Food Handling Regulations	22
Chapter 5: Location, Location, Location	**25**
Choosing the Perfect Spot for Your Pizzeria	25
Assessing Foot Traffic and Visibility	26
Negotiating Lease Agreements	27
Chapter 6: Building Your Brand	**31**
Developing a Memorable Brand Identity	31
Designing Your Logo and Visuals	32
Crafting a Compelling Story Behind Your Pizzeria	33
Chapter 7: Setting Up Your Kitchen	**37**
Selecting Equipment and Suppliers	37
Designing an Efficient Layout	38

Hiring and Training Staff ... 39

Chapter 8: Sourcing Ingredients ... 43
Finding High-Quality Ingredients ... 43

Establishing Relationships with Suppliers ... 44

Ensuring Consistency and Freshness ... 45

Chapter 9: Menu Development and Pricing ... 49
Creating a Balanced Menu ... 49

Setting Competitive Prices ... 50

Incorporating Seasonal Specials ... 52

Chapter 10: Marketing and Promotion ... 55
Building Buzz Before Launch ... 55

Leveraging Social Media Platforms ... 56

Hosting Events and Promotions ... 58

Chapter 11: Opening Day and Beyond ... 61
Preparing for Your Grand Opening ... 61

Handling Challenges and Feedback ... 62

Strategies for Long-Term Success ... 63

Chapter 12: Growing Your Pizzeria ... 67
Expanding Your Menu and Services ... 67

Opening Additional Locations ... 69

Building Customer Loyalty Programs ... 70

Conclusion ... 73

Chapter 1:
Introduction

Just saying the word "pizza" can make your mouth water, right? It's amazing how something as simple as dough, sauce, and cheese can bring so much joy to people's lives. Whether it's a classic Margherita, a loaded Meat Lovers, or a trendy Vegan Supreme, pizza has a way of satisfying our cravings and bringing people together.

Now, you might be wondering, out of all the businesses you could start, why choose a pizzeria? Well, let me tell you, there are plenty of good reasons!

First off, pizza is universally loved. Seriously, who doesn't like pizza? It's like the one food that everyone can agree on. Whether you're young or old, meat-eater or vegetarian, pizza has something for everyone.

Then there's the creative aspect. Running a pizzeria isn't just about making dough and tossing toppings. It's about expressing yourself through food. You get to play around with flavors, try out new ingredients, and create pizzas that are as unique as you are.

Plus, there's something special about being a part of your community. Pizzerias aren't just places to grab a slice; they're gathering spots where friends and families come together to share a meal and make memories. By opening a pizzeria, you get to be a part of that, creating a space where people feel welcome and at home.

And let's not forget about the financial side of things. Pizza is big business, my friend. With the right approach, a pizzeria can be a pretty profitable venture. So not only do you get to do something you love, but you also get to make some dough (pun intended) while you're at it.

So, what can you expect from this guide? Well, we're going to cover everything you need to know to get your pizzeria up and running. From coming up with your concept and doing market research to figuring out all the legal stuff and finding the perfect location, we've got you covered.

We'll also talk about building your brand, setting up your kitchen, and marketing your pizzeria to the masses. Whether you're a seasoned pro or a total newbie, this guide will give you the tools and confidence you need to turn your pizza dreams into reality.

So get ready to roll up your sleeves, because we're about to embark on an exciting journey filled with dough, sauce, and plenty of cheesy goodness. Welcome to the world of pizza entrepreneurship!

Chapter 2:
Crafting Your Concept

In the bustling world of pizza, crafting a unique and compelling concept is key to standing out from the competition. From the type of pizza you serve to the ambiance of your pizzeria, every aspect of your concept plays a crucial role in attracting customers and building a loyal following. In this chapter, we'll delve into the process of defining your concept, finding your niche in the pizza market, deciding on your menu and specialties, and designing your unique selling proposition.

Finding Your Niche in the Pizza Market

In the vast and ever-evolving world of pizza, there's a multitude of flavors, styles, and culinary traditions to explore. From the iconic New York slice to the hearty Chicago deep dish and the rustic Neapolitan pie, the pizza landscape offers endless possibilities. However, in such a competitive market, it's crucial to find your niche to distinguish yourself from the crowd. Here are some strategies to help you discover your place in the pizza market:

Start by researching your local competition. Take note of the types of pizza they offer, their pricing strategies, and the demographics they target. This can help you identify gaps or areas where you can offer something unique.

Don't limit yourself to the traditional pizza styles. While classics like New York and Neapolitan are popular, there's growing interest in lesser-known styles such as Detroit-style, Chicago deep dish, and artisanal wood-fired pizzas. You could also specialize in a specific regional cuisine, like Sicilian or Roman-style pizza, to appeal to customers seeking authentic flavors.

Consider catering to dietary preferences. With more people adopting gluten-free, vegan, and keto diets, offering alternative pizza options can attract a wider audience. Whether it's gluten-free crusts, vegan cheese, or keto-friendly toppings, accommodating various dietary needs can set you apart.

Get creative with your toppings and flavor combinations. Experiment with unconventional ingredients, seasonal specials, and themed pizzas to keep your menu fresh and exciting. Offering unique and memorable pizzas can help you stand out and attract attention.

Focus on using high-quality ingredients. Emphasize the freshness, authenticity, and origins of your ingredients to appeal to customers who prioritize quality. Whether it's locally sourced produce, artisanal cheeses, or homemade sauces, showcasing the quality of your ingredients can set you apart from chain restaurants and fast-food joints.

By implementing these strategies and finding your unique niche in the pizza market, you can differentiate yourself from competitors and attract a loyal customer base. With creativity, attention to detail, and a commitment to quality, your pizzeria can thrive in the bustling pizza scene.

Deciding on Your Menu and Specialties

Once you've identified your niche within the pizza market, the next step is to craft a menu that perfectly complements your concept and entices your target audience. Your menu serves as the face of your pizzeria, showcasing your unique offerings and setting the tone for the dining experience you aim to provide.

Keeping it simple is key to streamlining operations and ensuring consistency. While it may be tempting to offer an extensive array of pizzas to cater to every palate, simplicity often reigns supreme. Focus on a select number of signature pizzas that best exemplify your concept and allow you to showcase your culinary creativity. By highlighting a few standout options, you can help customers navigate your menu with ease and ensure that each pizza receives the attention it deserves.

At the same time, it's essential to strike a balance by offering enough variety to appeal to a diverse customer base. Incorporate a mix of classic favorites, specialty pizzas, and customizable options to cater to different tastes and preferences. Whether it's traditional pepperoni and margherita pizzas or unique creations featuring unexpected flavor combinations, providing a diverse selection ensures that there's something for everyone on your menu.

Embrace the bounty of each season by incorporating seasonal ingredients and flavors into your menu. Create limited-time specials and seasonal menus that capitalize on the freshest produce and ingredients available. Not only does this add excitement and variety to your offerings, but it also showcases your commitment to quality and seasonality. By regularly updating your menu to reflect the changing seasons, you can keep customers intrigued and coming back for more.

While pizza may be the star of the show, don't overlook the opportunity to complement your menu with a variety of other offerings. Consider including appetizers, salads, desserts, and beverages to provide a well-rounded dining experience. By offering a diverse selection of menu items, you can cater to different preferences and dietary restrictions while enhancing the overall dining experience for your customers. Additionally, offering a range of options beyond pizza can increase the likelihood of repeat visits and encourage customers to explore all that your pizzeria has to offer.

In conclusion, creating a standout pizza menu involves striking a balance between simplicity, variety, and seasonality while considering the diverse preferences of your target audience. By focusing on a select number of signature pizzas, offering a diverse selection of options, incorporating seasonal ingredients, and providing a complete dining experience, you can create a menu that sets your pizzeria apart and leaves a lasting impression on your customers.

Designing Your Unique Selling Proposition

In a crowded market, having a strong unique selling proposition (USP) is paramount for attracting customers and fostering brand loyalty. Your USP is what distinguishes your pizzeria from competitors and provides customers with a compelling reason to choose your establishment over others. Here are some effective strategies for designing a compelling USP:

Firstly, highlight your specialty. Whether it's a unique pizza style, a signature topping combination, or a special cooking technique, ensure that what makes your pizzeria distinctive takes center stage. This should serve as the focal point of your branding and marketing efforts, setting you apart in the minds of consumers.

Secondly, emphasize quality and freshness. If your pizzeria prioritizes premium ingredients and freshness, effectively communicate this to your customers. Showcase your sourcing practices, cooking methods, and any certifications or accolades that validate your commitment to delivering top-notch quality.

Thirdly, offer exceptional service. Outstanding service can be a potent differentiator in the competitive restaurant landscape.

Whether it's friendly and attentive staff, prompt and efficient service, or personalized touches that make guests feel valued, prioritize providing an unparalleled customer experience that keeps patrons returning.

Additionally, create a unique atmosphere. The ambiance and vibe of your pizzeria can significantly influence customer perceptions and set you apart from the competition. Whether you opt for a cozy neighborhood spot, a chic urban eatery, or a themed restaurant with a quirky concept, ensure that your space reflects your brand identity and resonates with your target audience.

Lastly, stand for something. In today's socially conscious era, many consumers are drawn to businesses that espouse values beyond mere profit-making. Consider aligning your pizzeria with a cause or ethos that resonates with your target demographic, whether it's sustainability, community engagement, or supporting local producers. Demonstrating a genuine commitment to something larger than yourself can foster a deeper connection with customers and engender loyalty.

By implementing these strategies and crafting a compelling USP, you can effectively differentiate your pizzeria in a crowded market, attract customers, and build a strong and enduring brand presence.

By carefully crafting your concept, menu, and unique selling proposition, you can position your pizzeria for success in a competitive market. Stay true to your vision, listen to your customers, and always be willing to adapt and evolve as you grow. With passion, creativity, and a commitment to excellence, you can build a pizzeria that delights customers and leaves a lasting impression in the world of pizza.

Chapter 3:
Market Research and Planning

In the world of entrepreneurship, success often hinges on thorough research and meticulous planning. Before diving headfirst into the exciting journey of starting your own pizzeria, it's essential to take the time to understand the market landscape, identify your target audience, and develop a comprehensive business plan. In this chapter, we'll explore the importance of market research and planning in setting the foundation for your pizzeria's success.

Analyzing the Local Market

The foundation of launching a successful pizzeria begins with conducting a thorough analysis of the local market. By gaining insights into the competitive landscape, understanding consumer preferences, and assessing economic trends in your area, you can develop a strategic business plan that maximizes your chances of success. Here's how to conduct market research effectively:

Identify Competitors:
Start by identifying existing pizzerias and other food establishments in your vicinity. Take note of their location, menu offerings, pricing, and customer reviews. By studying your competitors, you can gain a better understanding of the local pizza scene, assess the level of competition, and identify gaps or opportunities in the market.

Evaluate Demand:
Gauge the demand for pizza in your area by observing foot traffic at existing pizzerias, conducting surveys or focus groups with local residents, and analyzing demographic data. Consider factors such as population density, income levels, and dining habits to estimate the potential customer base for your pizzeria. Understanding the demand for pizza in your target market will help you tailor your

offerings to meet customer preferences and maximize sales potential.

Assess Trends:
Stay abreast of current trends and developments in the food industry, particularly those related to pizza and casual dining. Keep an eye on emerging flavor profiles, dietary preferences, and consumer behavior trends that may influence your menu offerings and marketing strategy. By staying attuned to industry trends, you can position your pizzeria to capitalize on evolving consumer preferences and stay ahead of the competition.

Consider Location:
The location of your pizzeria can significantly impact its success. Evaluate potential locations based on factors such as visibility, accessibility, parking availability, and proximity to residential and commercial areas. Conduct a thorough site analysis to identify high-traffic areas with strong demographic profiles that align with your target customer base. Choosing the right location is crucial for attracting customers and maximizing sales potential.

By conducting comprehensive market research, you can gain valuable insights that will inform your business strategy and increase the likelihood of launching a successful pizzeria. By understanding the competitive landscape, assessing demand, staying abreast of industry trends, and selecting the optimal location, you can position your pizzeria for long-term success in the dynamic and competitive food industry.

Understanding Your Target Audience

Once you've gained a clear understanding of the local market, the next critical step is to identify and comprehend your target audience. Understanding who your customers are, what they desire, and how to effectively connect with them is paramount for developing a successful marketing strategy and tailoring your offerings to meet their needs.

To define your target audience effectively, start with demographic analysis. Conduct a thorough examination of demographic data, including age, gender, income level, and household size, to profile your target audience. Additionally, consider factors such as family status, lifestyle preferences, and cultural background that may influence their dining choices. This analysis provides insights into the composition of your customer base, enabling you to tailor your offerings accordingly.

Dive deeper into psychographic profiling to understand the values, interests, attitudes, and behaviors of your target audience. Explore their dining habits, preferences, and motivations for choosing a pizzeria. By understanding the psychographic profile of your audience, you can craft messaging and promotions that resonate with their preferences and lifestyle, fostering stronger connections with your customers.

Engage directly with your target audience through surveys, focus groups, or interviews to gather feedback. Pose questions about their pizza preferences, dining habits, and expectations from a pizzeria to gain valuable insights into their needs and preferences. This direct engagement provides firsthand knowledge that informs your menu offerings, marketing strategies, and overall business approach.

Monitor social media platforms and online review sites to listen to conversations about pizza and dining experiences in your area. Pay attention to trends, complaints, and customer feedback to identify areas for improvement and opportunities for differentiation. By staying informed about customer sentiment, you can adapt your offerings and marketing efforts to better meet their needs and preferences.

By diligently defining and understanding your target audience, you can develop a nuanced understanding of their preferences, needs, and behaviors. Armed with this knowledge, you can craft targeted marketing strategies, tailor your menu offerings, and create a dining experience that resonates with your audience, ultimately driving customer satisfaction and loyalty.

Creating a Business Plan

With a clear understanding of the local market and your target audience, it's time to translate your vision into a comprehensive business plan. A well-crafted business plan serves as a roadmap for your pizzeria, outlining your goals, strategies, and financial projections. Here's what to include in your business plan:

Executive Summary: Provide a concise overview of your pizzeria concept, target market, competitive analysis, and financial projections. Summarize the key highlights of your business plan and outline your goals and objectives.

Company Description: Describe your pizzeria concept, including your mission statement, vision, and values. Provide details about your business structure, ownership, and legal status, as well as any unique features or advantages that set your pizzeria apart.

Market Analysis: Present your findings from the market research conducted earlier, including an analysis of the local market, competitor landscape, and target audience demographics. Identify market trends, opportunities, and threats that may impact your pizzeria's success.

Marketing and Sales Strategy: Outline your marketing and sales strategy for attracting customers and generating revenue. Define your branding, positioning, and promotional tactics, as well as your pricing strategy, distribution channels, and sales projections.

Operations Plan: Detail the day-to-day operations of your pizzeria, including staffing requirements, kitchen layout, equipment needs, and supply chain management. Outline your procedures for food preparation, customer service, inventory management, and quality control.

Financial Projections: Present detailed financial projections for your pizzeria, including startup costs, revenue forecasts, operating expenses, and cash flow projections. Include a break-even analysis and contingency plans for different scenarios to assess the feasibility and profitability of your business.

Appendices: Include any additional information or supporting documents that may be relevant to your business plan, such as market research data, menu concepts, resumes of key team members, or lease agreements.

By conducting thorough market research and creating a comprehensive business plan, you'll be well-equipped to navigate the challenges and opportunities of starting your own pizzeria. Stay true to your vision, adapt to changing market conditions, and always keep the needs of your target audience in mind. With careful planning and execution, you'll be on your way to building a successful and thriving pizzeria that delights customers and contributes to the vibrant culinary landscape of your community.

Chapter 4:
Legalities and Regulations

Starting a pizzeria involves more than just perfecting your dough recipe and creating mouthwatering toppings. It also requires navigating a complex web of permits, licenses, and regulations to ensure that your business operates legally and safely. In this chapter, we'll delve into the various legalities and regulations that pizzeria owners need to be aware of, including obtaining permits and licenses, complying with health and safety standards, and understanding food handling regulations.

Navigating Permits and Licenses

Before you can open your pizzeria to the public, you'll need to obtain the necessary permits and licenses to operate legally. The specific permits and licenses required may vary depending on your location, but here are some common ones to consider:

Business License: A business license is a basic requirement for operating any business legally. It authorizes you to conduct business in a specific location and ensures that you comply with local regulations and zoning laws. You can obtain a business license from your city or county government office.

Food Service Permit: If you're serving food to the public, you'll need a food service permit from your local health department. This permit ensures that your kitchen and food handling practices meet health and safety standards. To obtain a food service permit, you may need to undergo an inspection of your kitchen facilities and demonstrate compliance with sanitation requirements.

Alcohol License: If you plan to serve alcohol at your pizzeria, you'll need to obtain an alcohol license or permit from your state's alcohol control board. The requirements for obtaining an alcohol license may vary depending on your location and the type of alcohol you intend to serve (e.g., beer and wine only or full liquor service).

Sign Permit: If you plan to install outdoor signage for your pizzeria, such as a storefront sign or a banner, you may need to obtain a sign permit from your local government. Sign permits regulate the size, placement, and design of outdoor signs to ensure compliance with zoning laws and aesthetic standards.

Music License: If you plan to play music in your pizzeria, whether through live performances, recorded music, or streaming services, you may need to obtain a music license from performance rights organizations such as ASCAP, BMI, or SESAC. These licenses ensure that you have the legal right to play copyrighted music in your establishment and compensate the artists and songwriters for their work.

Building Permits: If you're making any structural changes to your pizzeria, such as renovations or additions, you may need to obtain building permits from your local building department. Building permits ensure that your construction projects comply with building codes and safety regulations.

Complying with Health and Safety Standards

Maintaining a clean and sanitary environment is essential for ensuring the health and safety of your customers and employees. As a pizzeria owner, you'll need to comply with a variety of health and safety standards to prevent foodborne illnesses and ensure proper hygiene practices. Here are some key health and safety regulations to be aware of:

Food Safety Regulations: Food safety regulations govern all aspects of food handling, storage, preparation, and serving to prevent contamination and foodborne illnesses. These regulations may include guidelines for proper handwashing, food storage temperatures, cleaning and sanitizing procedures, and employee hygiene practices. Make sure to familiarize yourself with local health department regulations and undergo any required food safety training or certification programs.

Sanitation Requirements: Maintaining a clean and sanitary kitchen is essential for preventing cross-contamination and ensuring the safety of your food products. Develop and implement a cleaning and sanitizing schedule for your kitchen equipment, utensils, and food preparation surfaces. Regularly inspect your kitchen for cleanliness and address any sanitation issues promptly.

Pest Control: Pests such as rodents, insects, and flies can pose a serious health risk in food establishments. Implement a pest control program to prevent infestations and maintain a pest-free environment. This may include sealing entry points, storing food properly, and working with a licensed pest control provider to monitor and control pest activity.

Allergen Management: Food allergies are a growing concern for many consumers, and it's essential to take precautions to prevent cross-contact with allergens in your kitchen. Train your staff on proper allergen handling procedures, clearly label menu items containing common allergens, and implement protocols to prevent cross-contamination during food preparation and serving.

Employee Health and Hygiene: Ensure that your employees follow strict hygiene practices to prevent the spread of illness and contamination. This includes washing hands regularly, wearing clean uniforms and hairnets, and avoiding food handling when sick. Implement policies for reporting illness and provide paid sick leave to encourage employees to stay home when they're unwell.

Understanding Food Handling Regulations

Proper food handling is critical for maintaining the quality and safety of your food products and preventing foodborne illnesses. As a pizzeria owner, you'll need to comply with food handling regulations set forth by local health departments and regulatory agencies. Here are some key regulations to be aware of:

Temperature Control: Proper temperature control is essential for preventing the growth of harmful bacteria and ensuring the safety of your food products. Monitor and record temperatures regularly to ensure that food is stored, cooked, and served at safe temperatures. Refrigerate perishable foods promptly and avoid leaving food at room temperature for extended periods.

Food Storage: Store food properly to prevent contamination and spoilage. Use a first-in, first-out (FIFO) system to rotate food stock and ensure that older items are used before newer ones. Store raw meats separately from ready-to-eat foods to prevent cross-contamination, and use proper food storage containers to maintain freshness and quality.

Cooking and Holding Temperatures: Cook food to the appropriate internal temperatures to ensure that it's safe to eat. Use food thermometers to verify that meats, poultry, and seafood reach the recommended minimum cooking temperatures. Hold hot foods at 135°F (57°C) or above and cold foods at 41°F (5°C) or below to prevent bacterial growth.

Cross-Contamination Prevention: Take precautions to prevent cross-contamination between raw and ready-to-eat foods. Use separate cutting boards, utensils, and preparation areas for raw meats and other ingredients. Wash hands, utensils, and surfaces thoroughly between tasks to avoid transferring bacteria from one food to another.

Personal Hygiene: Ensure that your employees follow strict personal hygiene practices to prevent the spread of illness and contamination. Provide handwashing stations with soap and warm water, and enforce frequent handwashing among staff. Encourage employees to wear clean uniforms, hairnets, and gloves when handling food, and prohibit behaviors such as smoking or eating in food preparation areas.

Navigating the legalities and regulations of starting a pizzeria requires careful attention to detail and compliance with a variety of requirements. By obtaining the necessary permits and licenses, complying with health and safety standards, and understanding food handling regulations, you can ensure that your pizzeria operates legally and safely. Stay informed about local regulations and best practices, and be proactive in addressing any compliance issues that may arise. By prioritizing legal and regulatory compliance, you can build a solid foundation for the success of your pizzeria and provide a safe and enjoyable dining experience for your customers.

Chapter 5:
Location, Location, Location

Choosing the perfect location for your pizzeria is one of the most critical decisions you'll make as a business owner. The right location can significantly impact your pizzeria's success, influencing factors such as foot traffic, visibility, accessibility, and overall profitability. In this chapter, we'll explore the importance of choosing the perfect spot for your pizzeria, assessing foot traffic and visibility, and negotiating lease agreements to secure the ideal location for your business.

Choosing the Perfect Spot for Your Pizzeria

When selecting a location for your pizzeria, numerous factors must be carefully weighed to ensure the success of your business. Here are several key considerations to keep in mind:

Target Audience:
It's crucial to consider the demographics and preferences of your target audience when choosing a location. Are you catering to families, students, professionals, or tourists? Select a location that aligns with the preferences and needs of your intended customer base. For instance, a pizzeria targeting families might benefit from locating near residential neighborhoods or schools.

Competition:
Evaluate the level of competition in the area and strategize how your pizzeria will distinguish itself. Look for locations with high demand for pizza but limited existing competition. Alternatively, consider positioning your pizzeria in close proximity to complementary businesses that attract a similar customer base, allowing for cross-promotional opportunities.

Accessibility:

Ensure that your pizzeria is easily accessible to your target audience. Choose a location with ample parking or convenient public transportation options to facilitate customer visits. This aspect is particularly crucial for pizzerias focusing on takeout and delivery services, as customers should find it hassle-free to collect their orders.

Visibility:
Aim for a location with high visibility to attract passing foot and vehicular traffic. Seek out spots with excellent signage opportunities and high exposure to maximize visibility and draw attention to your pizzeria. Locations near busy intersections, shopping centers, or tourist attractions tend to offer optimal visibility and foot traffic.

Surrounding Businesses:
Consider the neighboring businesses and amenities when selecting a location. Are there complementary businesses nearby that can drive foot traffic to your pizzeria? Look for areas with a diverse mix of retail, entertainment, and dining establishments to create a vibrant and bustling environment. Collaborating with nearby businesses can also foster mutually beneficial partnerships and promotions.

By carefully considering these factors, you can choose a location that not only meets the needs and preferences of your target audience but also provides the visibility, accessibility, and competitive advantage necessary for your pizzeria to thrive.

Assessing Foot Traffic and Visibility

Foot traffic and visibility are two key factors that can significantly impact the success of your pizzeria. Here's how to assess foot traffic and visibility when choosing a location:

Conduct Observations: Spend time observing foot traffic patterns in different potential locations at various times of day and week. Pay attention to peak hours, busy days, and seasonal fluctuations to get a sense of the area's foot traffic patterns.

Analyze Traffic Counts: Use data from local transportation departments or traffic monitoring services to assess vehicular traffic volume in the area. Higher traffic volumes can indicate greater visibility and exposure for your pizzeria.

Evaluate Pedestrian Flow: Evaluate the flow of pedestrians in the area, paying attention to pedestrian corridors, sidewalks, and pedestrian-friendly amenities such as benches or outdoor seating areas. Choose a location with a steady flow of foot traffic to maximize visibility and exposure.

Consider Surrounding Landmarks: Take note of surrounding landmarks, attractions, and points of interest that may draw visitors to the area. Locations near popular tourist attractions, cultural venues, or major employers may experience higher foot traffic and visibility.

Assess Signage Opportunities: Evaluate signage opportunities in potential locations to ensure that your pizzeria is visible and easy to find. Look for locations with prominent storefronts, ample window space, and opportunities for exterior signage to maximize visibility from the street.

Negotiating Lease Agreements

Once you've pinpointed a suitable location for your pizzeria, the subsequent pivotal step involves negotiating a lease agreement with the property owner or landlord. Here are some essential tips to navigate lease negotiations effectively:

Firstly, understand your needs. Before delving into lease negotiations, clearly outline your requirements and priorities for the space. Consider aspects like lease term, rent amount, renewal options, and any tenant improvement allowances or incentives that could benefit your business.

Secondly, seek professional assistance. It's prudent to enlist the expertise of a real estate attorney or leasing agent to guide you through lease negotiations. These professionals can navigate the intricacies of lease agreements, negotiate favorable terms on your behalf, and ensure that your interests are safeguarded throughout the process.

Thirdly, conduct research on comparable properties. Take the time to investigate similar properties in the area to ascertain market rental rates, prevalent lease terms, and tenant incentives. Armed with this information, you can negotiate a lease agreement that aligns with industry standards while meeting your business's financial objectives.

Next, engage in thorough negotiations. Be prepared to negotiate key lease terms such as rent amount, lease duration, security deposit, and tenant improvement allowances. Work collaboratively with the landlord to secure terms that are mutually beneficial and conducive to the success of your pizzeria.

Additionally, meticulously review the lease agreement. Prior to signing any documents, carefully scrutinize the lease agreement to ensure that all terms and conditions are clearly articulated and understood. Pay particular attention to clauses pertaining to rent escalation, maintenance responsibilities, lease renewal options, and any restrictions that may impact your operations.

Lastly, seek legal advice. It's advisable to consult with a real estate attorney to review the lease agreement and provide insights on any legal implications or concerns. A legal advisor can offer valuable guidance, elucidate your rights and obligations under the lease, and identify potential risks or pitfalls that warrant attention.

By adhering to these guidelines and approaching lease negotiations with diligence and foresight, you can secure a lease agreement that lays a solid foundation for the success of your pizzeria venture.

By carefully assessing foot traffic and visibility, negotiating lease agreements, and choosing a location that aligns with your target audience and business needs, you can set your pizzeria up for success. Remember that finding the perfect location may take time and effort, but the investment is well worth it in the long run. With the right location, your pizzeria can become a beloved fixture in the community and a go-to destination for pizza lovers near and far.

Chapter 6:
Building Your Brand

In the competitive world of pizzerias, building a strong and memorable brand is essential for standing out from the crowd, attracting customers, and fostering loyalty. Your brand is more than just a logo or a name; it's the essence of your pizzeria—the personality, values, and promise that you communicate to your customers. In this chapter, we'll explore the process of building your brand, including developing a memorable brand identity, designing your logo and visuals, and crafting a compelling story behind your pizzeria.

Developing a Memorable Brand Identity

Your brand identity is the visual and emotional representation of your pizzeria that communicates who you are and what you stand for. Developing a memorable brand identity involves defining your brand's personality, values, and unique attributes. Here's how to develop a strong brand identity for your pizzeria:

Define Your Brand Personality: Start by defining the personality traits and characteristics that you want your brand to embody. Is your pizzeria fun and quirky, elegant and sophisticated, or laid-back and casual? Consider how you want your brand to be perceived by customers and what emotions you want to evoke.

Identify Your Brand Values: Identify the core values and beliefs that guide your pizzeria's operations and decisions. Are you committed to using locally sourced ingredients, supporting sustainable practices, or providing exceptional customer service? Your brand values should align with your mission and resonate with your target audience.

Establish Your Brand Voice: Define the tone and voice that you'll use to communicate with your audience across various touchpoints, including your website, social media, and marketing materials. Whether it's friendly and conversational, authoritative and informative, or playful and humorous, your brand voice should reflect your brand personality and values.

Conduct Market Research: Conduct market research to understand your target audience's preferences, attitudes, and perceptions of your brand. Gather feedback through surveys, focus groups, or interviews to gain insights into what resonates with your audience and how you can tailor your brand identity to meet their needs.

Stay Consistent: Consistency is key to building a strong brand identity. Ensure that your brand's visual elements, messaging, and customer experience are cohesive and aligned across all channels and touchpoints. Consistent branding helps build brand recognition and reinforces your brand's identity in the minds of customers.

Designing Your Logo and Visuals

Your logo and visual identity are crucial elements of your brand identity that help convey your brand's personality and create a memorable impression. Here's how to design a logo and visuals that represent your pizzeria effectively:

Define Your Design Aesthetic: Start by defining the design aesthetic and visual style that best represents your brand. Consider factors such as color palette, typography, imagery, and overall aesthetics. Choose visual elements that align with your brand personality and resonate with your target audience.

Hire a Professional Designer: Consider hiring a professional graphic designer or branding agency to create your logo and visual identity.

A skilled designer can translate your brand vision into compelling visual elements that capture the essence of your pizzeria and differentiate you from competitors.

Focus on Simplicity and Versatility: Aim for a logo and visual identity that are simple, versatile, and easily recognizable. Your logo should be scalable and legible across various applications and sizes, from signage and packaging to digital platforms and social media profiles.

Incorporate Meaningful Elements: Incorporate visual elements and design elements that convey the unique attributes and values of your pizzeria. Whether it's a symbol, icon, or typography, choose elements that have meaning and relevance to your brand story and resonate with your audience.

Test and Iterate: Once you've developed initial concepts for your logo and visual identity, test them with your target audience to gather feedback and insights. Iterate on your designs based on feedback, making refinements and adjustments as needed to ensure that your visual identity effectively represents your brand.

Crafting a Compelling Story Behind Your Pizzeria

Crafting a compelling brand story is essential for connecting with your audience on a deeper level and standing out in a crowded market. Here's how you can create a captivating narrative for your pizzeria:

Firstly, start with your why. What inspired you to open your pizzeria? Maybe it's your love for authentic Italian cuisine or a desire to bring people together over delicious food. Whatever it is, sharing your passion and purpose behind your pizzeria helps customers connect with your brand on a more personal level.

Secondly, highlight your unique selling proposition. What makes your pizzeria different from the rest? Whether it's your secret family recipes, commitment to using fresh, locally sourced ingredients, or exceptional customer service, emphasize what sets you apart and why customers should choose you over other options.

Next, showcase your heritage and values. Share the story behind your pizzeria, including its origins, traditions, and core values. Whether you're a family-owned business with a rich history in pizza-making or a modern pizzeria with a focus on innovation and sustainability, your heritage and values shape your brand's identity and resonate with customers.

Humanize your brand by putting a face to your pizzeria. Share stories about the people behind the scenes—the passionate chefs, dedicated staff, and loyal customers who make your pizzeria special. Highlighting their experiences and contributions adds a personal touch to your brand and helps customers feel more connected to your business.

Be authentic and transparent in your storytelling. Share both your successes and challenges openly with your audience. Authenticity builds trust and credibility with customers, fostering stronger relationships and loyalty over time.

Finally, engage your audience in your brand story. Encourage customers to share their own experiences and stories with your pizzeria, whether through social media, online reviews, or in-person interactions. Creating opportunities for interaction and participation helps foster a sense of community and belonging around your brand, turning customers into loyal advocates.

By crafting a compelling brand story that resonates with your audience, you can create an emotional connection, differentiate your pizzeria from competitors, and build long-lasting brand loyalty.

In conclusion, building a strong brand is essential for the success of your pizzeria and requires careful consideration of your brand identity, logo and visuals, and brand story. By developing a memorable brand identity that reflects your pizzeria's personality and values, designing compelling visuals that create a lasting impression, and crafting a compelling brand story that resonates with your audience, you can build a strong brand that stands the test of time and fosters loyalty among customers. Stay true to your brand's essence, engage with your audience authentically, and continuously refine and evolve your brand to stay relevant and competitive in the dynamic world of pizzerias.

Chapter 7:
Setting Up Your Kitchen

Setting up your kitchen is a pivotal step in launching your pizzeria successfully. A well-equipped kitchen, efficient layout, and skilled staff are essential for delivering delicious pizzas and providing excellent service to your customers. In this chapter, we'll delve into the process of setting up your kitchen, including selecting equipment and suppliers, designing an efficient layout, and hiring and training staff to ensure smooth operations and exceptional quality.

Selecting Equipment and Suppliers

Choosing the right equipment is critical for the success of your pizzeria. From ovens and mixers to prep tables and refrigeration units, each piece of equipment plays a vital role in your kitchen's functionality and productivity. Here's how to select the right equipment and suppliers for your pizzeria:

Assess Your Menu Needs: Start by assessing your menu and determining the equipment you'll need to execute your recipes efficiently. Consider the types of pizzas you'll be offering, as well as any additional menu items such as salads, appetizers, or desserts. Make a list of essential equipment based on your menu requirements.

Research Equipment Options: Research different equipment options available on the market, considering factors such as quality, durability, efficiency, and cost. Look for reputable suppliers and manufacturers known for producing high-quality equipment designed specifically for pizzerias and foodservice establishments.

Consider Space Constraints: Take into account the size and layout of your kitchen space when selecting equipment. Choose equipment that fits comfortably within your kitchen's footprint and allows for efficient workflow and maneuverability. Consider space-saving options such as countertop appliances or stackable units to maximize space utilization.

Prioritize Essential Equipment: Prioritize essential equipment that is critical for pizza production, such as pizza ovens, dough mixers, dough presses, and refrigeration units. Invest in high-quality equipment for your core operations to ensure consistency, reliability, and durability.

Evaluate Supplier Options: Research different suppliers and vendors to find the best options for purchasing your equipment. Consider factors such as pricing, warranties, customer service, and delivery options when evaluating suppliers. Establish relationships with reliable suppliers who can provide ongoing support and maintenance for your equipment.

Designing an Efficient Layout

The layout of your kitchen plays a crucial role in determining the efficiency and productivity of your operations. A well-designed layout minimizes wasted space, optimizes workflow, and promotes smooth coordination among kitchen staff. Here's how to design an efficient layout for your pizzeria kitchen:

Plan Your Workflow: Start by mapping out the workflow of your kitchen, from receiving and storage to preparation, cooking, and plating. Identify the key steps involved in each stage of production and arrange your equipment and workstations accordingly to minimize movement and maximize efficiency.

Separate Work Zones: Divide your kitchen into distinct work zones based on the different tasks and functions performed. Designate separate areas for dough preparation, topping assembly, baking, and finishing to streamline operations and prevent cross-contamination.

Create a Logical Flow: Arrange your equipment and workstations in a logical sequence that follows the natural flow of production. Position equipment and supplies in the order they are used, with minimal movement between stations. Consider factors such as proximity, accessibility, and safety when designing your layout.

Optimize Space Utilization: Maximize the use of available space in your kitchen by utilizing vertical space, incorporating multi-functional equipment, and implementing space-saving storage solutions. Arrange equipment and workstations efficiently to minimize clutter and congestion and create clear pathways for staff to move around.

Ensure Safety and Compliance: Design your kitchen layout with safety and compliance in mind, ensuring that it meets health and safety regulations and industry standards. Allow adequate space between equipment and workstations to prevent accidents and injuries, and ensure proper ventilation and exhaust systems to maintain air quality and temperature control.

Hiring and Training Staff

Your kitchen staff forms the backbone of your pizzeria, playing a pivotal role in delivering the quality and consistency that keep customers coming back. Hiring and training skilled personnel are crucial steps in maintaining high standards and providing exceptional service. Here's how you can effectively recruit and train staff for your pizzeria kitchen:

Start by clearly defining job roles and responsibilities for each position in your kitchen. From pizza chefs to prep cooks and dishwashers, outline the specific duties, qualifications, and expectations for each role. Developing detailed job descriptions will help streamline the hiring process and ensure that candidates understand what is required of them.

When recruiting candidates, seek out individuals with relevant experience, skills, and qualifications for the positions you're looking to fill. Utilize online job boards, social media platforms, and industry-specific networks to attract qualified applicants. Consider conducting interviews and skills assessments to assess candidates' suitability for the role and ensure they align with your kitchen's needs.

Once you've hired new staff members, provide comprehensive training to familiarize them with your kitchen operations, equipment, recipes, and food safety protocols. Offer a combination of hands-on training sessions, demonstrations, and written materials to ensure that employees are equipped with the knowledge and skills they need to excel in their roles.

Encourage a collaborative and supportive work environment in your kitchen by fostering teamwork, communication, and mutual respect among staff members. Promote a positive culture that values collaboration, creativity, and continuous improvement. By creating a supportive atmosphere, you'll boost morale and productivity among your kitchen team.

Invest in ongoing development opportunities for your kitchen staff to enhance their skills, knowledge, and performance. Offer cross-training opportunities, skills workshops, and professional development programs to help employees grow and advance in their careers. Providing avenues for growth and development will not only benefit your staff but also contribute to the overall success of your pizzeria.

Finally, provide regular feedback and recognition to acknowledge staff members' contributions and provide constructive guidance for improvement. Recognize and reward exceptional performance, teamwork, and dedication to motivate your staff and foster a positive work culture. By showing appreciation for your employees' hard work and dedication, you'll inspire loyalty and create a supportive and thriving work environment in your pizzeria kitchen.

Setting up your kitchen involves carefully selecting equipment and suppliers, designing an efficient layout, and hiring and training skilled staff to execute your recipes with precision and consistency. By investing in high-quality equipment, designing an efficient workflow, and cultivating a skilled and motivated team, you can create a kitchen environment that promotes productivity, creativity, and excellence. Stay committed to maintaining high-quality standards, continuous improvement, and fostering a positive work culture to ensure the success and sustainability of your pizzeria kitchen.

42

Chapter 8:
Sourcing Ingredients

Sourcing high-quality ingredients is fundamental to the success of any pizzeria. The quality of your ingredients directly impacts the taste, texture, and overall experience of your pizzas. In this chapter, we'll explore the importance of sourcing top-notch ingredients, establishing relationships with suppliers, and ensuring consistency and freshness in your ingredient sourcing process.

Finding High-Quality Ingredients

The quest for high-quality ingredients begins with a commitment to sourcing the best possible products for your pizzeria. Whether it's the tomatoes in your sauce, the cheese on your pizzas, or the flour in your dough, each ingredient contributes to the final product's flavor and quality. Here are some key considerations for finding high-quality ingredients:

Freshness: Choose ingredients that are fresh and in season whenever possible. Fresh ingredients not only taste better but also retain more nutrients and flavor compared to their processed or preserved counterparts. Visit local farmers' markets, specialty grocers, and artisanal producers to find fresh, locally sourced ingredients for your pizzas.

Quality: Invest in high-quality ingredients that meet your standards for taste, texture, and appearance. Look for ingredients that are free from additives, preservatives, and artificial flavors or colors. Choose premium ingredients such as imported cheeses, specialty meats, and organic produce to elevate the quality of your pizzas.

Authenticity: Embrace authenticity in your ingredient sourcing process, seeking out traditional and artisanal products that reflect the authentic flavors and culinary traditions of Italy. Choose authentic Italian ingredients such as San Marzano tomatoes, buffalo mozzarella, and extra virgin olive oil to add depth and authenticity to your pizzas.

Sustainability: Consider the environmental and ethical impact of your ingredient choices, opting for sustainably sourced and ethically produced ingredients whenever possible. Choose ingredients that are produced using environmentally friendly practices, support local farmers and producers, and prioritize fair trade and ethical labor practices.

Flavor Profile: Pay attention to the flavor profile of your ingredients and how they complement each other in your pizzas. Experiment with different varieties of tomatoes, cheeses, meats, and herbs to find the perfect balance of flavors for your signature pizzas. Consider incorporating unique and exotic ingredients to add complexity and depth to your menu offerings.

Establishing Relationships with Suppliers

Building strong relationships with suppliers is essential for ensuring reliable access to high-quality ingredients and fostering trust and collaboration in your ingredient sourcing process. Cultivating relationships with trusted suppliers allows you to negotiate favorable terms, access specialty products, and receive personalized service and support. Here's how to establish relationships with suppliers:

Research Suppliers: Research potential suppliers and vendors to find reputable partners who offer the ingredients you need at competitive prices. Consider factors such as product quality, reliability, delivery options, and customer service when evaluating suppliers.

Visit Suppliers: Take the time to visit potential suppliers in person to tour their facilities, meet their team, and sample their products. Building a personal connection with suppliers allows you to assess their operations firsthand and ensure that they meet your quality and ethical standards.

Communicate Your Needs: Clearly communicate your ingredient requirements, preferences, and expectations to your suppliers. Provide detailed specifications for each ingredient, including quality standards, packaging requirements, and delivery schedules. Establish open lines of communication to address any issues or concerns promptly.

Negotiate Terms: Negotiate terms and pricing with your suppliers to ensure that you receive fair and competitive pricing for your ingredients. Consider factors such as volume discounts, payment terms, and exclusivity agreements when negotiating contracts with suppliers.

Build Trust and Collaboration: Foster trust and collaboration in your relationships with suppliers by being transparent, reliable, and responsive. Maintain open communication, provide feedback and constructive criticism, and work together to resolve any challenges or issues that arise.

Ensuring Consistency and Freshness

Consistency and freshness are key factors in delivering high-quality pizzas that meet customer expectations every time. By implementing proper inventory management, storage practices, and quality control measures, you can ensure that your ingredients are consistently fresh and of the highest quality. Here's how to ensure consistency and freshness in your ingredient sourcing process:

Inventory Management: Implement effective inventory management practices to monitor ingredient levels, track usage, and minimize waste. Use inventory management software or systems to streamline ordering, receiving, and tracking of ingredients, ensuring that you have the right ingredients on hand when you need them.

Just-In-Time Ordering: Adopt a just-in-time ordering approach to minimize inventory holding costs and ensure freshness. Order ingredients from suppliers based on your production schedule and projected demand to maintain optimal freshness and minimize waste.

Proper Storage: Store ingredients properly to maintain freshness and prevent spoilage. Follow storage guidelines provided by suppliers and manufacturers, and ensure that ingredients are stored at the appropriate temperature and humidity levels to preserve their quality.

Quality Control: Implement quality control measures to monitor the quality and freshness of your ingredients throughout the sourcing process. Conduct regular inspections and sensory evaluations of ingredients to identify any signs of spoilage, contamination, or deterioration.

Rotate Stock: Practice first-in, first-out (FIFO) inventory rotation to ensure that older ingredients are used before newer ones. Rotate stock regularly to minimize the risk of spoilage and ensure that ingredients remain fresh and of the highest quality.

Train Staff: Train your kitchen staff on proper ingredient handling and storage procedures to ensure that ingredients are handled safely and hygienically. Educate staff on the importance of freshness and quality control in delivering exceptional pizzas to customers.

By sourcing high-quality ingredients, establishing relationships with trusted suppliers, and implementing proper quality control measures, you can ensure that your pizzeria delivers consistently fresh and delicious pizzas that delight customers every time. Stay committed to sourcing the best possible ingredients, maintaining strong supplier relationships, and upholding high-quality standards to set your pizzeria apart from the competition and build a loyal customer base.

Chapter 9:
Menu Development and Pricing

Menu development and pricing are essential aspects of running a successful pizzeria. A well-crafted menu not only showcases your culinary offerings but also influences customers' dining decisions and contributes to your restaurant's profitability. In this chapter, we'll explore the process of creating a balanced menu, setting competitive prices, and incorporating seasonal specials to keep your offerings fresh and enticing.

Creating a Balanced Menu

A balanced menu is one that offers a diverse selection of dishes that appeal to a wide range of tastes and preferences while maintaining a cohesive theme and consistent quality. When developing your pizzeria's menu, consider factors such as variety, dietary preferences, portion sizes, and pricing. Here's how to create a balanced menu:

Variety: Offer a variety of pizza styles, toppings, and flavor combinations to cater to different preferences and dietary restrictions. Include classic favorites such as Margherita and Pepperoni pizzas alongside specialty creations featuring unique ingredients and flavor profiles.

Dietary Preferences: Accommodate diverse dietary preferences and restrictions by offering vegetarian, vegan, gluten-free, and dairy-free options on your menu. Clearly label menu items with dietary symbols or descriptions to make it easy for customers to identify suitable choices.

Portion Sizes: Offer a range of portion sizes to accommodate different appetites and dining occasions. In addition to individual-sized pizzas, consider offering larger sharing sizes for groups or families, as well as smaller sizes for appetizers or light meals.

Appetizers and Side Dishes: Enhance your menu with a selection of appetizers, salads, and side dishes that complement your pizzas and offer additional variety. Include options such as garlic knots, bruschetta, salads, and pasta dishes to provide a well-rounded dining experience.

Beverage Selection: Round out your menu with a diverse selection of beverages, including soft drinks, craft beers, wines, and specialty cocktails. Offer non-alcoholic options such as house-made lemonades, iced teas, and artisanal sodas to cater to all tastes.

Seasonal Specials: Incorporate seasonal ingredients and flavors into your menu to keep it fresh and exciting year-round. Create seasonal specials featuring locally sourced produce, seasonal toppings, and limited-time offerings that capitalize on current culinary trends and seasonal flavors.

Setting Competitive Prices

Setting competitive prices is a critical aspect of running a successful pizzeria, as it directly impacts your ability to attract customers, drive sales, and achieve profitability. Here's a comprehensive guide on how to set competitive prices for your menu items:

Cost Analysis: Start by conducting a thorough cost analysis to determine the true cost of each menu item. This analysis should include factors such as ingredient costs, labor expenses, overhead, and other operational costs. Calculate your food cost percentage and desired profit margin to establish a pricing structure that covers your expenses while still generating a reasonable profit.

Competitive Analysis: Research competitor pricing in your local market to understand prevailing price points for similar menu items. Take note of portion sizes, ingredient quality, and service offerings when comparing prices with competitors. This insight will help you position your prices competitively while still offering value to your customers.

Value Perception: Consider the perceived value of your menu items from the customer's perspective. Price your items based on the perceived quality, uniqueness, and desirability of the ingredients and preparations. Highlight value-added features such as premium ingredients, artisanal preparations, and generous portion sizes to justify higher prices and differentiate your offerings from competitors.

Pricing Strategy: Develop a pricing strategy that balances profitability with competitiveness and value. Explore options such as tiered pricing for different menu categories, bundle deals and combo meals, and promotional pricing for limited-time offers or specials. Your pricing strategy should align with your target market and business objectives while maximizing revenue opportunities.

Menu Engineering: Utilize menu engineering techniques to strategically position high-profit items and drive sales. Highlight profitable menu items with strategic placement, visual cues, and enticing descriptions to encourage upselling and increase overall revenue. Regularly review and adjust your menu layout and presentation to optimize profitability.

Monitor and Adjust: Continuously monitor sales performance and gather customer feedback to evaluate the effectiveness of your pricing strategy. Stay informed about changing market conditions, customer preferences, and cost fluctuations, and be prepared to adjust your prices accordingly to maintain competitiveness and profitability. Regularly reviewing and adjusting your pricing strategy will ensure that your pizzeria remains competitive and financially sustainable in the long run.

By following these steps and adopting a strategic approach to pricing, you can set competitive prices for your menu items that attract customers, maximize sales, and drive profitability for your pizzeria.

Incorporating Seasonal Specials

Seasonal specials offer an opportunity to showcase fresh, seasonal ingredients, experiment with new flavors and recipes, and create excitement among customers. By incorporating seasonal specials into your menu, you can keep your offerings dynamic and relevant while capitalizing on seasonal trends and flavors. Here's how to incorporate seasonal specials into your menu:

Seasonal Ingredients: Take advantage of seasonal produce, meats, and other ingredients to create seasonal specials that highlight the flavors of each season. Incorporate fresh, locally sourced ingredients that are in peak seasonality to maximize flavor and quality.

Culinary Trends: Stay informed about current culinary trends and seasonal flavor profiles to inspire your seasonal specials. Experiment with trending ingredients, flavor combinations, and cooking techniques to create innovative and on-trend offerings that resonate with customers.

Limited-Time Offers: Introduce limited-time offers and promotions to generate excitement and urgency around your seasonal specials. Offer exclusive menu items, prix fixe menus, or seasonal tasting menus for a limited time to encourage customers to try something new and unique.

Menu Refresh: Use seasonal specials as an opportunity to refresh your menu and introduce new menu items. Rotate seasonal specials regularly to keep your menu fresh and encourage repeat visits from customers eager to try the latest offerings.

Promote Seasonal Specials: Promote seasonal specials through your marketing channels, including your website, social media, email newsletters, and in-store signage. Use enticing food photography, descriptive language, and limited-time offers to create buzz and drive sales.

Gather Feedback: Solicit feedback from customers about your seasonal specials to gauge their popularity and effectiveness. Use customer feedback to refine your seasonal offerings, fine-tune recipes, and make adjustments based on customer preferences.

By creating a balanced menu that offers variety, accommodates dietary preferences, and incorporates seasonal specials, you can appeal to a wide range of customers and keep them coming back for more. Set competitive prices that reflect the value of your offerings while remaining profitable, and regularly monitor and adjust your pricing strategy to stay competitive in the market. Incorporate seasonal specials to keep your menu fresh and exciting, and capitalize on seasonal trends and flavors to delight your customers and drive sales.

Chapter 10:
Marketing and Promotion

Marketing and promotion are essential components of launching and sustaining a successful pizzeria. Effective marketing strategies help build awareness, attract customers, and drive sales, while promotions and events create excitement and encourage customer engagement. In this chapter, we'll explore the process of building buzz before launch, leveraging social media platforms, and hosting events and promotions to market your pizzeria effectively.

Building Buzz Before Launch

Building buzz before your pizzeria's launch is a crucial step in ensuring a successful opening day. Here's how you can generate excitement and anticipation among potential customers:

Teaser Campaigns: Create teaser campaigns to spark curiosity and anticipation. Use social media, email newsletters, and your website to share sneak peeks of menu items, behind-the-scenes photos, or countdowns to opening day. Teasers build anticipation and keep potential customers eagerly awaiting your grand opening.

Social Media Teasers: Leverage the power of social media platforms to share updates and build excitement. Post photos and videos of your pizzeria's progress, including construction, menu development, and staff training. Engage with followers by asking for their input on menu items or inviting them to vote on pizza names, creating a sense of involvement and anticipation.

Engage Influencers: Partner with local influencers, bloggers, and food enthusiasts to expand your reach and generate buzz. Invite influencers to exclusive preview events or offer them complimentary tastings in exchange for sharing their experiences with their followers. Their endorsement can help build credibility and excitement around your pizzeria.

Local PR Outreach: Reach out to local media outlets and publications to generate press coverage for your launch. Offer story ideas, press releases, and media kits to pitch your pizzeria as an exciting addition to the local dining scene. Press coverage can help generate awareness and attract attention from potential customers.

Community Engagement: Get involved in the local community to build goodwill and support for your pizzeria. Consider sponsoring local events, participating in fundraisers, or hosting community gatherings to connect with residents and businesses. Building relationships with the community can create loyal customers and advocates for your brand.

By implementing these strategies and building buzz before your pizzeria's launch, you can generate excitement, attract attention, and ensure a successful opening day. Creating anticipation among potential customers sets the stage for a memorable debut and lays the foundation for long-term success.

Leveraging Social Media Platforms

Social media platforms are powerful tools for marketing and promoting your pizzeria, allowing you to connect with customers, showcase your offerings, and build a loyal following online. With strategic planning and creative content, you can leverage social media to drive engagement, increase brand awareness, and drive sales. Here's how to leverage social media platforms effectively:

Establish a Presence: Create profiles on popular social media platforms such as Instagram, Facebook, Twitter, and TikTok to establish a presence for your pizzeria online. Use consistent branding, including your logo, colors, and imagery, to create a cohesive and recognizable identity across platforms.

Share Visual Content: Use high-quality photos, videos, and graphics to showcase your pizzas, menu items, and behind-the-scenes moments on social media. Post mouthwatering photos of your pizzas, videos of chefs in action, and behind-the-scenes glimpses of your kitchen to engage and entice your audience.

Engage with Followers: Actively engage with your followers by responding to comments, messages, and mentions promptly. Encourage dialogue and interaction by asking questions, soliciting feedback, and running polls and contests to spark engagement and foster a sense of community.

Utilize Hashtags: Use relevant hashtags to increase the visibility of your social media posts and reach a broader audience. Research popular hashtags related to pizza, food, and your local area, and incorporate them into your posts to attract new followers and drive engagement.

Run Promotions and Giveaways: Run promotions, giveaways, and exclusive offers on social media to incentivize engagement and reward your followers. Offer discounts, freebies, and special deals to followers who like, comment, or share your posts, or run contests and giveaways to generate excitement and participation.

Collaborate with Influencers: Partner with influencers, food bloggers, and local tastemakers to amplify your social media reach and exposure. Collaborate with influencers to create sponsored content, host takeover events, or feature guest posts on your social media channels to reach new audiences and gain credibility and authenticity.

Hosting Events and Promotions

Hosting events and promotions is an effective way to drive foot traffic, generate buzz, and create memorable experiences for your customers. From grand opening celebrations to weekly specials and themed events, there are countless opportunities to engage with your audience and drive sales through events and promotions. Here's how to host events and promotions effectively:

Grand Opening Celebration: Host a grand opening celebration to mark the launch of your pizzeria and attract a crowd of eager customers. Offer special promotions, discounts, and giveaways to entice guests, and create a festive atmosphere with music, entertainment, and food tastings.

Weekly Specials: Offer weekly specials and promotions to keep customers coming back for more. Whether it's a "Pizza of the Week" featuring a rotating selection of specialty pizzas or a "Happy Hour" promotion offering discounts on drinks and appetizers, weekly specials create excitement and drive sales.

Themed Events: Host themed events and promotions to capitalize on holidays, seasonal trends, and cultural celebrations. Whether it's a Valentine's Day pizza dinner, a Halloween costume party, or a summer pizza and beer festival, themed events provide opportunities for creativity, engagement, and customer interaction.

Loyalty Programs: Implement a loyalty program to reward repeat customers and encourage repeat visits. Offer incentives such as points, discounts, and exclusive perks for members who frequent your pizzeria regularly. Use digital loyalty apps or punch cards to track customer purchases and reward loyalty.

Collaborative Events: Partner with other local businesses, organizations, or charities to host collaborative events and promotions. Team up with nearby breweries for a pizza and beer pairing event, collaborate with a local charity for a fundraising dinner, or partner with a neighboring business for a cross-promotional event.

Online Ordering Promotions: Encourage online orders and takeout/delivery sales by offering exclusive promotions and discounts for customers who order through your website or mobile app. Offer incentives such as free delivery, discounts on first orders, or loyalty points for online orders to drive online sales and increase customer convenience.

By building buzz before launch, leveraging social media platforms, and hosting events and promotions, you can effectively market and promote your pizzeria, attract customers, and drive sales. Stay engaged with your audience, listen to their feedback, and adapt your marketing strategies and promotions to meet their needs and preferences. With a strategic approach to marketing and promotion, your pizzeria can thrive and become a beloved destination in your community.

Chapter 11:
Opening Day and Beyond

Opening day marks the culmination of months, if not years, of planning, preparation, and anticipation. It's the moment when your pizzeria officially opens its doors to the public, inviting customers to experience your culinary creations and hospitality for the first time. However, the journey doesn't end on opening day—it's just the beginning of a new chapter in your pizzeria's story. In this chapter, we'll explore the process of preparing for your grand opening, handling challenges and feedback, and implementing strategies for long-term success as you embark on your journey beyond opening day.

Preparing for Your Grand Opening

Preparing for your grand opening involves a multitude of tasks that demand meticulous planning, attention to detail, and a focus on delivering an unforgettable experience for your customers. In the days leading up to the big event, it's essential to finalize menu offerings, train your staff, conduct test runs, and market your opening to the community effectively. Here's how you can prepare for your grand opening:

First and foremost, ensure that your menu offerings are meticulously curated, reflecting the essence of your pizzeria's concept and vision. Take the time to finalize menu items, ensuring they are well-balanced and cohesive. Conduct menu tastings and staff training sessions to familiarize your team with the menu and ensure they're equipped to answer any customer inquiries.

Invest in comprehensive training for your staff to ensure they deliver exceptional service that aligns with your pizzeria's standards. Provide training on various aspects, including customer service, food preparation, safety protocols, and POS systems. Well-trained staff can elevate the overall dining experience and leave a lasting impression on customers.

Conduct test runs and soft openings to identify and address any operational issues or challenges before your grand opening. Invite friends, family, and trusted patrons to dine at your pizzeria during these trial runs, soliciting feedback on the food, service, and overall experience. Addressing any issues early on can help ensure a smooth and successful opening day.

Generate excitement and anticipation for your grand opening by marketing it to the community through various channels. Utilize social media platforms, email newsletters, local advertising, and grassroots outreach to spread the word and attract customers to your pizzeria on opening day. Engage with the community and build anticipation through strategic marketing efforts.

Consider offering special promotions, discounts, or giveaways to incentivize customers to visit your pizzeria on opening day. Create enticing offers such as complimentary appetizers or desserts with the purchase of a pizza, or exclusive discounts for customers who mention your grand opening promotion. These special offers can help drive foot traffic and generate buzz for your grand opening festivities.

Handling Challenges and Feedback

Despite careful planning and preparation, challenges and feedback are inevitable when opening a new pizzeria. Whether it's addressing operational issues, managing customer expectations, or responding to negative feedback, how you handle challenges and feedback can significantly impact your pizzeria's reputation and success. Here's how to handle challenges and feedback effectively:

Stay Calm and Flexible: Stay calm and flexible in the face of challenges and unexpected obstacles that arise during the opening process. Approach each challenge with a problem-solving mindset, and be willing to adapt and adjust your plans as needed to overcome obstacles and maintain operations.

Listen to Customer Feedback: Actively listen to customer feedback and take it seriously, whether it's positive or negative. Use customer feedback as an opportunity to identify areas for improvement, address concerns, and make necessary adjustments to enhance the customer experience.

Respond Promptly and Professionally: Respond promptly and professionally to customer inquiries, complaints, or feedback, whether it's in person, over the phone, or online. Acknowledge the customer's concerns, apologize for any inconvenience, and offer a solution or resolution to address their issue.

Empower Your Staff: Empower your staff to handle customer complaints and resolve issues independently whenever possible. Provide them with the authority, training, and support they need to address customer concerns and ensure that they feel empowered to provide exceptional service.

Use Feedback to Improve: Use feedback from customers, staff, and stakeholders to identify areas for improvement and implement changes to enhance your operations and customer experience. Continuously monitor feedback, analyze trends, and make data-driven decisions to drive continuous improvement.

Strategies for Long-Term Success

Beyond the excitement of opening day, the key to long-term success lies in your ability to sustain momentum, adapt to changing market conditions, and cultivate a loyal customer base.

Implementing strategic initiatives and focusing on building relationships with customers and the community are essential for long-term success. Here are some strategies for long-term success:

Maintain Consistency: Maintain consistency in your product quality, service standards, and overall customer experience to build trust and loyalty among customers. Consistency creates reliability and predictability, ensuring that customers know what to expect every time they visit your pizzeria.

Build Relationships: Build meaningful relationships with customers, suppliers, and the local community to foster loyalty and support for your pizzeria. Engage with customers on social media, participate in community events, and support local charities and organizations to connect with the community and build goodwill.

Monitor Performance Metrics: Monitor key performance metrics such as sales, customer satisfaction, and repeat business to track your pizzeria's performance and identify areas for improvement. Use data analytics and POS systems to gather insights into customer behavior and preferences, and use this information to make informed decisions about your operations and marketing strategies.

Adapt to Market Trends: Stay abreast of industry trends, consumer preferences, and market dynamics to adapt your menu offerings, marketing strategies, and operations accordingly. Embrace innovation, experimentation, and creativity to stay ahead of the curve and differentiate your pizzeria in a competitive market.

Seek Feedback and Continuous Improvement: Continuously seek feedback from customers, staff, and stakeholders to identify opportunities for improvement and innovation. Encourage open communication, listen to feedback, and implement changes based on customer preferences and market trends to stay relevant and competitive.

In conclusion, opening day marks the beginning of a new chapter in your pizzeria's journey, but it's just the first step in a long and rewarding adventure. By preparing diligently, handling challenges and feedback effectively, and implementing strategies for long-term success, you can position your pizzeria for sustained growth, profitability, and success in the months and years ahead. Stay focused on delivering exceptional experiences, building relationships with customers, and continuously improving your operations to create a thriving and beloved pizzeria that stands the test of time.

Chapter 12:
Growing Your Pizzeria

Growing your pizzeria is an exciting yet challenging endeavor that requires strategic planning, innovation, and a commitment to delivering exceptional experiences to your customers. Whether you're expanding your menu and services, opening additional locations, or implementing customer loyalty programs, each growth opportunity presents its own set of opportunities and challenges. In this chapter, we'll explore strategies for growing your pizzeria and taking your business to the next level.

Expanding Your Menu and Services

Expanding your menu and services is a strategic move that can bring numerous benefits to your pizzeria. By offering a wider variety of menu options and additional services, you not only attract new customers but also increase revenue and set yourself apart from competitors. Here's an in-depth look at various strategies for expanding your menu and services:

Introduce New Menu Items: One of the most straightforward ways to expand your menu is by regularly introducing new and innovative offerings. Experiment with unique pizza toppings, specialty pies, appetizers, salads, and desserts to keep your menu fresh and exciting. By continually adding new items, you can keep customers interested and eager to try something new each time they visit.

Offer Customization Options: Give your customers the freedom to personalize their dining experience by offering customization options. Provide a variety of crusts, sauces, and toppings so that customers can create their perfect pizza combination. Customization not only enhances customer satisfaction but also allows you to cater to a wider range of tastes and preferences.

Expand Beyond Pizza: While pizza may be the star of your menu, consider diversifying your offerings by incorporating additional menu categories. Add pasta dishes, sandwiches, wraps, or desserts to appeal to customers looking for alternative options. Don't forget to include vegetarian, vegan, and gluten-free choices to accommodate diverse dietary needs and attract new customer segments.

Provide Catering Services: Extend your services beyond your pizzeria by offering catering for events, parties, and corporate functions. Develop catering packages and customizable menus tailored to different occasions and group sizes. Catering services not only generate additional revenue streams but also help you establish relationships with corporate clients and expand your customer base.

Implement Online Ordering and Delivery: In today's digital age, offering online ordering and delivery services is essential for meeting customer expectations and staying competitive. Partner with third-party delivery platforms or develop your own in-house delivery system to reach customers beyond your immediate area. Online ordering and delivery increase convenience for customers and open up new revenue opportunities for your pizzeria.

Host Cooking Classes or Workshops: Engage with your customers and community members by hosting cooking classes or workshops. Teach participants how to make pizza at home through hands-on instruction, cooking demonstrations, and tastings. Not only does this allow you to showcase your culinary expertise, but it also strengthens customer loyalty and reinforces your brand's authority in the realm of pizza-making.

Expanding your menu and services requires careful planning and execution, but the benefits—such as attracting new customers, increasing revenue, and enhancing the overall dining experience—are well worth the effort. By implementing these strategies, you can position your pizzeria for long-term success and growth in a competitive market.

Opening Additional Locations

Expanding your pizzeria by opening additional locations is a significant milestone that offers opportunities for growth, increased market reach, and economies of scale. However, it also presents challenges such as managing multiple locations, maintaining consistency, and ensuring brand integrity. Here are some strategies for opening additional locations successfully:

Conduct Market Research: Conduct thorough market research to identify viable locations for expansion based on demographics, competition, foot traffic, and market demand. Evaluate factors such as population density, income levels, and consumer preferences to determine the suitability of potential locations.

Develop a Growth Strategy: Develop a comprehensive growth strategy that outlines your expansion goals, target markets, timeline, and resource requirements. Determine whether you'll pursue organic growth through company-owned locations or franchise opportunities to scale your business efficiently.

Standardize Operations: Standardize your operations, processes, and procedures to ensure consistency and quality across multiple locations. Develop standardized recipes, training programs, and operational guidelines to maintain uniformity and uphold your pizzeria's brand standards.

Hire and Train Staff: Invest in hiring and training staff for your new locations to ensure that they embody your pizzeria's culture, values, and commitment to excellence. Provide comprehensive training on food preparation, customer service, and operational procedures to equip staff with the skills they need to succeed.

Implement Scalable Systems: Implement scalable systems and technologies to support the growth of your pizzeria's operations. Invest in POS systems, inventory management software, and other tools that streamline operations, improve efficiency, and facilitate communication across multiple locations.

Foster Community Engagement: Foster community engagement and local connections at each new location to establish a presence in the community and build customer loyalty. Participate in local events, sponsorships, and partnerships to connect with residents and businesses and promote your pizzeria as a valued member of the community.

Building Customer Loyalty Programs

Building customer loyalty is essential for retaining existing customers, driving repeat business, and maximizing customer lifetime value. Implementing customer loyalty programs is an effective way to incentivize repeat purchases, reward loyal customers, and foster long-term relationships with your patrons. Here are some strategies for building customer loyalty programs:

Develop a Loyalty Program: Develop a customer loyalty program that rewards customers for their repeat business and incentivizes them to return to your pizzeria regularly. Offer rewards such as discounts, freebies, exclusive offers, or points-based rewards that customers can redeem for future purchases.

Offer Tiered Rewards: Offer tiered rewards or loyalty levels that incentivize customers to spend more and earn additional benefits. Create different membership tiers based on customer spending or visit frequency, and offer escalating rewards and perks as customers progress through the tiers.

Personalize Rewards and Offers: Personalize rewards and offers based on individual customer preferences, purchase history, and behavior. Use customer data and insights to tailor promotions, discounts, and rewards to each customer's unique tastes and preferences, enhancing their loyalty and engagement.

Encourage Referrals and Reviews: Encourage customers to refer their friends and family to your pizzeria by offering referral incentives or rewards. Encourage satisfied customers to leave positive reviews and testimonials on review sites, social media, and other platforms to build credibility and attract new customers.

Communicate Regularly: Communicate regularly with loyalty program members to keep them engaged and informed about special offers, promotions, and events. Send personalized emails, SMS messages, or push notifications to update members on their rewards status, upcoming promotions, and exclusive offers.

Measure and Analyze Results: Measure the effectiveness of your loyalty program by tracking key performance metrics such as customer retention, repeat purchase rate, and average order value. Analyze data and feedback to identify trends, assess program performance, and make data-driven decisions to optimize your loyalty program's effectiveness.

In conclusion, growing your pizzeria requires strategic planning, innovation, and a commitment to delivering exceptional experiences to your customers. Whether you're expanding your menu and services, opening additional locations, or implementing customer loyalty programs, each growth opportunity presents its own set of challenges and opportunities. By implementing strategic initiatives, fostering customer loyalty, and maintaining a focus on quality and consistency, you can successfully grow your pizzeria and achieve long-term success in a competitive market.

Conclusion

The journey of starting and growing a pizzeria is filled with excitement, challenges, and opportunities. Throughout this guide, we've explored the various aspects of launching a pizzeria, from crafting your concept and conducting market research to navigating legalities, selecting a location, and building your brand. We've delved into the importance of sourcing high-quality ingredients, designing a balanced menu, and setting competitive prices to attract customers and drive sales.

As you embark on your journey, it's essential to remain adaptable, resilient, and customer-focused. Embrace feedback, learn from challenges, and continuously strive for improvement to create a pizzeria that delights customers and stands out in a competitive market. Whether you're preparing for your grand opening, expanding your menu and services, opening additional locations, or building customer loyalty programs, each step forward brings you closer to achieving your goals.

Remember that success in the pizzeria industry is not just about serving delicious pizza—it's about creating memorable experiences, fostering community connections, and building lasting relationships with customers. Stay true to your vision, uphold your values, and maintain a commitment to quality, consistency, and excellence in everything you do.

As you navigate the highs and lows of entrepreneurship, remember that you're not alone. Seek guidance from mentors, connect with fellow pizzeria owners, and surround yourself with a supportive team who shares your passion and dedication. Together, you can overcome challenges, celebrate successes, and create a pizzeria that becomes a beloved institution in your community.

Above all, enjoy the journey. Starting and growing a pizzeria is a labor of love, but it's also a rewarding and fulfilling pursuit. Cherish the moments of triumph, celebrate milestones, and savor the joy of bringing people together over a delicious slice of pizza. With perseverance, creativity, and a commitment to excellence, your pizzeria can thrive and become a cherished destination for pizza lovers near and far.

www.ingramcontent.com/pod-product-compliance
Lightning Source LLC
Chambersburg PA
CBHW070407230526
45471CB00006B/2688